101 Ways to Play with a 3-year-old

Nanook Books

ISBN 978-1-62321-096-0

Nanook Books

www.nanookbooks.com

New York 2013

101 Ways to Play with a 3-year-old

Cover design by
Magda Lena Rook

Elaborated by
Dena Angevin, Anne Jackle, Mariola Langowski,
Betty Lucky, Ben Torrent

Illustrated by
Jack Beetle, Patricia Gazda

Typesetting by
Magda Lena Rook

Nanook Books

Intro

The third year of life is an interesting period in the development of your child: he remembers more, has a more active imagination, listens willingly and tries to solve problems, but also knows how to oppose adults and older children. He has his own ideas and expects your approval in carrying them out. Your little one is able to accomplish many tasks: from playing with playground equipment to drawing and using scissors. This is the time for organising games at home, outside, one on one — with a parent — or with a group of other children.

The suggestions found within the pages of this book are adapted to the needs and abilities of the three-year-old. They will allow you to support your child's natural development and at the same time combine pleasure and principle: through play he will learn, for example, how to set the table or help with the shopping; you will strengthen family ties and show him how to collaborate with a group of his peers. All you need to play with a child is the will, time and invention — it doesn't take very much to bring joy to your little one and yourself. Have fun!

A word about pronouns

He and she have been alternated throughout these activities, but every activity is for boys or girls!

Fun for one

Language lab

Group play

Outdoors fun

Manual dexterity

Make room for fun

Artistic invention

Physical activity

Powers of observation

Emotional intelligence at play

Do-it--yourself

Level of difficulty: * Easy ** Moderate *** Difficult

1
The Name Game

This is an activity that can be enjoyed anywhere: at home, at the park, in the doctor's waiting room or in a train. You might also find it useful to have a book with pictures. Point to the objects around you (or in the book) and say: "This is a couch, and this is..." Let your child finish the sentence. Make mistakes from time to time and let your child correct you — a task she will no doubt revel in! Other variations on this game include naming animals, colours or shapes.

---

* Your child learns to listen carefully and observe as well as enriches his or her vocabulary.

2
Hands Down

Prepare a few white sheets of paper, special paints for body painting, water in a plastic container and a sponge. Ask your child to choose a paint colour and then, using a sponge, apply it to the palms of his hand. Have him press down firmly on the paper, then lift and see the handprints left behind. Do it again...and again, because children love to make handprints! This is a good time to teach your child the names of each finger of the hand.

---

* Releases creativity and imagination; requires concentration and accuracy.

3
Tomato

A fun activity for a group of children. One randomly chosen child asks the others questions, to which they should reply with one word only: "Tomato!" These questions can be ordinary, such as "What are you doing?" or "What is your name?" or funny and tricky like "Why are you laughing?" If a child answers with another word or starts to laugh — that child forfeits a personal object (e.g. a sock, hair clip or a stuffed animal). Forfeited objects can be returned once the child says a rhyme or sings a song.

---

*   Develops a sense of humour and quick reflexes.

4

Bike Ride

Lay down with your child with your backs on the floor or a bed and the bottom of your feet touching each other. Start peddling with you feet, raising them slightly — first in slow motion and then faster and faster. Take a rest when you need to and then get right back on the 'bike' again!

---

*   Excellent exercise for the leg muscles.

5

A Crowning Moment

Draw a crown and cut it out. Lay it out on a piece of newspaper and ask your child to use glue and coloured glitter as decoration. Once the final touches are in place, staple the ends and place the crown on your child's head. Take a picture as a souvenir!

---

*   Increases manual dexterity and creative invention.

6
Let's Have a Party

Ask the child to invite dolls and other stuffed animals. Sit them on the floor, putting a plate in front of each 'guest' and in the middle a bowl with a variety of 'treats' — blocks, chestnuts, stones or other objects. When everything is ready, the party can begin: the host spins a spoon. When it stops, the handle side of the spoon indicates the guest who can eat. The winner is the one whose plate fills first. This game is even more fun if the guests include other children.

---

* A random game with very simple rules. It teaches a child about winning and losing.

7

What's in There?

Point to the child's room and ask: "What's in there?" "My room," might be the reply. "What's in your room?"; "A car."; "What's in the car?"; "The steering wheel." And so on. The questions and answers don't have to be serious. They can also be humorous or illogical: "What's in the car?"; "A hole."; "What's in the hole?"; "Mice."

This game can also be played away from home — in a car or outside.

---

* Teaches logical thinking, expands a child's vocabulary, and stimulates imagination and ingenuity.

8
Easter Egg

You will need pieces of coloured paper, a sheet of paper, glue and a pencil. Draw an egg on the paper. Let your child tear off pieces of coloured paper, roll them into balls and then glue them on the egg (which should be smeared liberally with glue). Continue until the egg is completely filled in. Three-year-olds can become impatient if a task lasts too long — if this should happen help your child finish this masterpiece.

---

*   Develops manual dexterity and teaches to recognise colours.

9

Two of a Kind

Fill a box with a variety of gloves — for winter, cleaning, gardening, etc. — in all different sizes. Give your child time to examine them and then pick out two identical gloves and explain the concept of a pair. Then let your child match the others and guess who wears each pair and why.

** Matching identical objects, understanding the concept of 'pair' and developing sentence formation.

10

"Airplane!"

Lay down on a blanket, pillow or carpet. Raise your legs and bend them slightly, then invite your child to lean his stomach against the soles of your feet. Holding the child's hands, lift your child into the air. Once your child feels more confident, try to briefly let go of his hands. Another variation of this game involves rocking your child forward and backward on your feet.

---

* Excellent exercise for parent and child.

11
Old Bear

For this game you will need a musical instrument. A toy that makes music will work, but you can also use household items like tin pans, empty containers or chopsticks. Ask all the children to sit in a circle around the child who is chosen to be the 'bear'. The bear guards the instrument, which represents a pot of honey.

The children say this rhyme:

Isn't it funny how bears like honey?
Buzz, buzz, buzz.
I wonder why he does.
Go to sleep, Mr. Bear.
Don't peep, Mr. Bear.

The 'bear' pretends to sleep and a child from the circle takes the 'honey pot', hiding it behind his or her back after making the instrument sound off. Then everyone shouts: "Wake up, Mr. Bear; someone has stolen your honey!" The bear has to guess who is hiding his honey pot based on where the sound was coming from and if he guesses correctly, the child who took it becomes the bear in the next round.

---

* An excellent exercise for honing listening skills.

12

Mirror, Mirror

Children love to make faces in front of the mirror. Have your child open her eyes wide, close them or wink. Ask your child to make faces that show emotion such as anger or surprise. Smile wide, stick out your tongue or show your teeth. There are countless scary, sad and happy faces to choose from! You can also pull your ears up, down or make them stand out. Join in and your child will have even more fun.

---

* Fantastic exercise for the face muscles; develops a child's creativity.

13

How Many Fingers

Put out your hand and hold up two fingers. Now ask your child to hold up the same number of fingers. One by one increase the number of fingers you are holding up and count: "One, two…" Reverse roles if your child is ready or ask her to count on her own. It's also a great opportunity for your child to show you how old she is.

** Teaches counting and showing one's age using fingers.

14

Stick Painting

Prepare a sheet of paper, paint, a stick and a piece of cotton. Wrap the cotton around the end of the stick. Explain to your child that cotton is absorbent and moves smoothly over paper. Ask your child to draw a picture!

---

* Teaches a new painting technique and develops the imagination.

15

Hello, Hello!

This is a game for two children who should stand back to back at a distance of about half a foot, feet wide apart and arms at their sides. At the signal 'One, two, three!' both children should bend over, placing their hands flat on the floor. Staying in this position, the children should look at one another through the window of their legs and say: "Hello, hello!" At the next 'One, two, three!' the children should link hands, and then let go before returning to a standing position. To make this game work, the children must coordinate their movements.

---

*   Great exercise for the entire body: strengthens the back muscles, stretches arm and leg muscles and teaches coordination, not to mention putting children in a good mood.

16

King and Court

Let the children choose a 'king'. This game is even more fun if you have prepared a paper crown in advance. The king makes gestures and describes them aloud. The other children, or courtiers, parrot the king's gestures and words. If, for example, the king says 'the king smiles', the children also smile and repeat the phrase 'the king smiles' all together. Let the children take turns being king. Gestures can include yawning, pointing a finger, scratching, etc. — everything depends on the creativity of the child.

---

*   This is a good game for developing language and acting skills: children learn to recite as a group and imitate gestures as well as practise creativity.

17

Ink Blots

Place a large drop of black or coloured ink on a piece of white cardboard paper on a flat surface. Let your child move the paper in any direction to create an unusual picture. Watch out for the table and floor — the ink should stay on the paper. If your child wants to make more images, get a fresh piece of paper and try other ink colours.

---

*   Your child learns a new way to create a picture, practises precise movements and uses imagination and creativity.

18

The Hokey Pokey

Create a circle on the ground with a string or a hula hoop — your child (or a group of children) will put parts of their body inside of the circle while singing the following rhyme:

> You put your right hand in.
> You put your right hand out.
> You put your right hand in
> And you shake it all about.
> You do the hokey pokey
> and you turn yourself around. (turn around outside of the circle)
> That's what it's all about. (clap three times on this line in rhythm)

Almost any body part will work: try feet, legs, arms, elbows, knees, head, stomach, even the tongue!

* This game develops a sense of rhythm and physical coordination as well as strengthens a child's sense of left and right.

19

Home Sweet Home

Building a house is a well-known game, one that even our grandmothers and their grandmothers played. Cover a table with a large piece of material (e.g. an old sheet) to imitate walls. Cut out holes to make windows and doors, and just like in a real house, create curtains and drapes. Decorate the house with your child in any way you see fit — inside or out.

---

* If you want to make your child very happy, create a permanent space for a house like this one — children like to have their own private 'haven'.

20
Name That Shadow!

Ask your child to sit across from a wall and behind her place a lamp — the light should fall on the opposite wall. Stand behind your child with an assortment of toys (dolls, stuffed animals, horses, etc.). One by one, place them in front of the light to create a shadow — make them move from side to side or dance. Have your child guess which toy the shadow belongs to. After three wrong answers, switch roles and let your child make some shadows for you!

---

* Your child learns observation skills and how to distinguish the shapes of different objects.

21

Over the Great Blue Sea

Draw pictures of islands and palm trees on cardboard paper and spread them out on a rug, spaced so that your child can walk or jump from one 'island' to the next. Now explain the game: the rug is the ocean, inhabited by hungry sharks, and the pieces of paper are safe 'islands' for your 'giant' to walk or jump to in crossing the ocean. Your child should avoid falling into the 'water'. If he does touch the rug, become a shark and pull him gently on the leg, pinching or tickling.

 ＊ Teaches controlled movement, balance and concentration.

22

Spider and Flies

While a group of children become 'flies', running and buzzing around the room, one child chosen to play the 'spider' waits in the corner. When you say 'spider', all of the children must freeze in place — like mannequins. The spider emerges from its hiding place and circulates around the room, inspecting the flies. If a fly laughs or moves and the spider sees it, that fly accompanies the spider back to his corner. The last 'fly' to escape capture wins the game!

---

*   Teaches patience and self-control.

23

What's That Animal?

Ask your child to imitate an animal, both the noises it makes and the way it moves. For example, if the animal is a dog, your child should bark (Woof! Woof!) and walk on four legs. Guess which animal your child is pretending to be and then switch roles.

---

*   Excellent exercise for a child in combination with the fun of imitation.

24
Massage

You can massage a child in a sitting or standing position, although the most comfortable position is probably for your child to lie down on his or her stomach. Read the poem below using the suggested movements. Take your time. This is a moment of relaxation for you and your child. Finish up with a big hug.

This is our park.
>Draw a square in the middle of the back.

This is the carousel turning in circles.
>Draw a circle inside the square, tracing gently with your index finger.

In each corner is a swing,
>Tap gently in each corner with your index finger.

and here are the sandbox and benches.
>Draw a square and a rectangle.

Through the middle is a path.
>Draw a squiggly line down the middle of the back.

This is our house,
>Draw a square at the end of the path, near the bottom of the back.

and a fence,
>Draw a fence in front of the square.

where a cat is climbing.
>Simulate climbing with the pads of your index and middle fingers.

"Look! It's starting to rain!
>Tap gently with the pads of your fingers, imitating rain.

Run home quickly,
>Run the pads of your index and middle fingers over the back.

because it's going to pour!"
>Tap harder with the pads of your fingers to imitate a downpour.

---

* A relaxing activity. Stroking and cuddling brings children a lot of happiness and gives parents an opportunity to show love through touch.

25

Mini Detective

Ask your child to look around the room and memorise everything he sees. Then ask him to leave. Move an object, starting with something large and characteristic. Invite your child back into the room and ask him to identify the difference. Alternate roles, letting your child move and find moved objects in turn. This is a game that never has to end!

** Develops spatial orientation and observation skills.

26

Make a Mushroom

Draw a mushroom on hard cardboard and cut it out. Let your child use this template to trace more mushrooms on a sheet of white paper. Next, have your child colour the caps red and use a tube of toothpaste to make white dots on them, before finally colouring the background green.

** An activity that develops muscle coordination and manual dexterity as well as precision.

27

What's That Sound?

Ask your child to sit down and close her eyes. Make different noises — walk loudly across the floor, tear a piece of paper, push the buttons on a toy phone, clap your hands, open and close the door to the room, knock on the door, wind a spinning top, play a toy instrument, turn on the radio. Have your child guess what is making the noise. Start with the simplest noises — those that your child already knows — and gradually increase the difficulty of the noises you make. Exchange roles.

** Your child exercises concentration and imagination as well as learns how to differentiate sounds.

28
Obstacle Course

Lay out blocks and pillows or cardboard boxes on the floor to create a small obstacle course. Mark the starting point and finish line using, for example, a line of blocks. Next to the finish line place your hand on a cardboard box — you will act as a bridge. Ask the child to choose a car and tackle the obstacle course, finishing by passing under your hand — or bridge — at the end.

---

*   Great physical activity.

29

What's Next?

Sing your child's favourite song or recite a poem and stop in the middle — your child will think you can't remember what comes next and should finish the rest. He or she will probably be proud to have a better memory than you do.

---

* Exercises listening memory and correct pronunciation.

30

I Am a Robot

Ask your child if he knows what a robot is. If not, explain that a robot is a machine that is able to move on its own and carry out tasks. Show how a robot moves, imitating the slow, precise movements of a robot's body and its voice. Tell your child that it is his turn to be a robot and carry out the tasks you set, for example, putting away crayons or another task your child doesn't like to do. He might think it isn't such a bad thing after all... or announce cleverly that the robot is broken! If the latter occurs, prepare a backup plan: fix the robot, pretending to rub it with oil and help it to carry out its 'mission impossible'.

---

* Teaches precision and control over one's body as well as develops the imagination.

31

Spring into Action

Have your child curl into a tiny ball on the floor. Now explain that your child is pretending to be a tiny seed. Pretend to water and shine sunlight on the 'seed', talking about how it is starting to grow, expanding its roots and reaching its leaves towards the sky. Once your child is standing tall, ask him or her to do it again, faster and faster until your child is leaping into the air.

---

*   Good physical activity that increases sensitivity to and curiosity about nature.

32

True or False?

Recount an interesting event from your child's life or make up an interesting story to tell. The subject should be easy to understand and concerning something that your child is familiar with. Every so often interrupt the story with a sentence that isn't true, such as 'sugar falls from the sky' or 'I saw a giraffe with a trunk', which the child can correct. Your child will be so proud to set you straight!

When you finish the story, let your child tell you a story so that you can play the part of the sceptical detective.

** Develops good listening skills and logical thinking as well as teaches a child to differentiate between what is true and false.

33

Red Light, Green Light!

This is an excellent game for playing outside. One child plays the 'stoplight' and the rest try to touch him or her. At the start, all the children form a line a good distance from the stoplight. The stoplight faces away from the line of kids and says: "Green light!" At this point the kids are allowed to move towards the stoplight. At any moment, the stoplight may say: "Red light!" and turn around. If any of the kids are caught moving after this has occurred, they are out. Play resumes when the stoplight turns back around and says: "Green light!" The stoplight wins if all the kids are out before anyone is able to touch him or her. Otherwise, the first player to touch the stoplight wins the game and earns the right to be 'stoplight' for the next round.

Green light!

---

* Teaches concentration and self-control as well as provides a chance to practise speed.

34
What if?

The rules are simple. Start by asking your child silly questions such as: What if elephants were pink? What if you could fly? What if our house was underground? Your child will probably jump at the chance to elaborate on these interesting ideas. Give your child a chance to ask some 'what if' questions that you can explore together. This is also a good activity to explore your child's fears or worries (e.g. about the dark, monsters under the bed or in the closet).

---

* Your child learns to use his imagination, be silly and also potentially explore fears or worries in a safe space. Moreover, this is a good bonding exercise with Mum or Dad.

35

One of a Kind

Cut out pictures of animals, fruits or other objects from colour magazines — the more different types of objects there are, the hardest this game will be! Your child's task is to choose one group of objects, for example animals. Have your child glue each picture belonging to the chosen group on a piece of white paper or cardboard.

***

** This activity develops manual dexterity, observation skills and the ability to associate facts.

36
Behind Enemy Lines!

Propose this game when your child has visitors! Collect all the balls or balloons in the house and create two team lines using string or ribbon on the floor. Divide the children into two teams, each of which stands behind its own 'line' with the balls or balloons lined up in front. When the children hear the phrase 'Behind enemy lines!' they take the balls or balloons and throw them across the other team's line (all the while staying behind their own). When you say the word 'Stop', the team with the fewest balls (or balloons) behind their own line wins.

---

* A great physical activity that trains reflexes.

Rock Painting

Prepare some paints and brushes and then set out in search of interesting rocks: in your own backyard, at a neighbourhood park, at the beach or in the woods. Give your child free rein in designing and painting the rocks. Your child has created her very own rock garden!

** Awakens your child's creativity and imagination as well as develops manual dexterity.

38
On the Roll

Have the children sit close together on the floor with their legs apart and feet touching those of the children on either side. Roll a ball into this circle, asking the children to catch the ball in turn and roll it to another child in the circle. The ball should move fluidly between players and stay inside the circle. After the children have mastered the game, add another ball and another. See how many balls the circle can keep moving at one time!

---

*   A good physical exercise that improves movement coordination
     and group cooperation as well as guarantees fun.

39

Blowing Bubbles

Pour dish soap into a large bowl of water and give your child a straw to place in the water and blow bubbles with. You can also use ready bubble liquid. If more than one child can play, this game is even more fun!

* This is a good speech therapy exercise.

40

Jack Be Nimble

This game is an adaptation of the famous nursery rhyme 'Jack be nimble, Jack be quick, Jack jump over the candlestick'. Have a group of children stand in a circle and place a small object like a beanbag in the centre. One by one call out each child's name and invite him or her to jump over the beanbag: e.g. "John be nimble, John be quick, John jump over the beanbag quick!"

** A great physical exercise for children, which develops body coordination, timing and a sense of rhythm.

41
Animal Collage

Find a picture of an animal in a colour magazine and cut it out. Glue the animal's body on one sheet of paper and its head on another. Now ask your young artist to use a crayon or marker to draw in the missing parts. Note to parents: you might be surprised at what your child creates — a three-year-old is still learning to draw and has a lot of creative ideas!

---

* Stimulates the imagination and develops creativity.

42

Fun with Faces

Cut out pictures of children's faces from a colour magazine picturing different emotions: joy, sadness, anger, surprise or fear. Ask your child to choose one picture and guess which emotion it shows. If the picture portrays a child with a big smile, ask your child why the child in the picture is happy — let her simply invent a story that explains the emotion.

---

*   Your child learns to recognise and name emotions.

43

Criss-Cross Applesauce

Ask your child to sit with his legs criss-crossed with his hands crossed behind his head. Next have him bend to the left, come back to the centre (sitting straight) and then bend to the right. Your child shouldn't use his arms or legs for help. Repeat this exercise a few times. Of course, if you exercise alongside your child, this becomes a lot more fun!

* Strengthens the muscles of the back and develops fluid movement as well as balance.

44

Funny Face

Everything you need to make this portrait can be found in your home: pieces of coloured material, string or cotton, buttons, plastic containers and carrots. Together with your child, lay all these materials out on a piece of paper to create a face. Buttons, for example, can be eyes, cotton can make eyebrows, hair or a mouth and a carrot can create a nose. Have fun experimenting!

---

*   Creative play: develops the imagination and awakens creativity.

45

Have a Ball!

Have your child sit on the floor, placing a ball between her ankles and holding it so it doesn't fall. The trick is to lift the ball in different directions: up and down, left and right; try a circle in the air. Let your child take a break and then repeat these movements again or create your own. The only rule is not to let the ball drop.

** A great developmental exercise overall — teaches body coordination and control.

46

Yarn Art

Prepare a piece of cardboard paper, yarn, watercolour paints, a small paint brush, scissors, glue and an old catalogue. Fold the paper in half twice until it is the size of a postcard. Cut on the folds to create four rectangles. Then ask your child to dip the yarn into the paint — the paintbrush might be handy here. Holding the dry end of the yarn, have your child lower it slowly onto the paper in whatever pattern he wants. Cover the first rectangle with a second one and put both of them inside the catalogue. Close the catalogue and, holding it shut firmly with your hand, ask your child to pull out the piece of yarn; this needs to be done rather quickly so the rectangles don't stick together. You can put this picture in a frame and use it to decorate your child's room.

** Develops imagination and manual dexterity. Creating such a unique piece of art will bring your child a lot of satisfaction.

47

Cooperative Musical Chairs

This is a variant of the traditional game in which children compete for a shrinking number of chairs. Ask the children to get into pairs and group the same number of chairs as there are pairs of children. Turn on the music and have the children walk around the chairs. When the music stops, the idea is for each pair to quickly sit down and share one of the chairs! Now remove one chair and the next musical round may begin. The pair that does not manage to secure a seat drops out of the game. After every round, remove one additional chair.

* Children train reflexes and reinforce the idea of cooperation within a pair.

48

Shape Up

Ask your child to cut out a variety of animal pictures out of a colour magazine and trim the pictures to reveal each animal's body shape. Glue the pictures onto cardboard paper — one animal on each sheet. Now ask your child to use a marker to draw contour lines around the animals. The first line should be closest to the picture and each one consecutively farther away until the entire page is filled.

---

*   An activity children enjoy and which develops precise movements of the hand — skills that are needed to learn to write.

49

Box Cars

To create the body, cut out the bottom of a cardboard box and tear off the flaps on the top. For your little driver, attach straps on opposite walls and it's ready for a test drive! The exhaust pipe can be made from cardboard paper and empty yogurt containers make excellent lights. Don't forget to make a license plate with your child's name on it. Once the car has been out on the open road, you and your child can also paint it together. Have fun!

* Creating this car with you brings your child a lot of joy and 'driving' it awakens the imagination and dreams of travelling.

50

My Mother Said…

Tell your child a story from your own childhood. From time to time interrupt the story with random commands, such as 'Scratch your nose', 'Point to your eye' or 'Lie down'. Before you give a command for your child to carry out, say the sentence: "My mother said…" Try to trick your child by changing the tone and rhythm of the story.

** This game requires good listening and comprehension skills.

51

Duck, Duck, Goose!

Gather a group of children and sit down in a circle. Have one child be the 'duck'. That person walks around the circle repeating 'duck-duck-duck' while tapping each person individually on the head. When the duck taps a child on the head and says 'goose', this child must jump up and try to catch the duck, while running around the circle. If the 'duck' gets around the circle and sits down in the space where the 'goose' was sitting, the goose becomes the duck in the next round.

---

* A game that hones flexibility, speed and reflexes as well as exposes a child to winning and losing.

52

Kids and Mummies

This is a game for two pairs, each of which receives a roll of coloured toilet paper to create a mummy. One child from each pair stands still while the other wraps him or her in toilet paper, avoiding the head. The pair that creates a mummy the fastest wins. Take of picture of both pairs as a souvenir.

** Very good exercise for the entire body, not to mention the great fun.

53

Get in Shapes

Cut out shapes from coloured paper: large and small circles, squares, triangles, rectangles and stars. Use them to create a simple design on the floor: a small circle, large circle, another small circle and another large circle. Ask your child to look at the sequence you have made and recreate it. Repeat the game and increase the difficulty by making other sequences.

** An excellent exercise for your child's memory.

54

At the Store

If you have to go to the store and your child doesn't want to accompany you, propose the following game. Start by preparing a shopping list: draw all of the products that you have to buy and explain clearly each sketch. Give your child this cheat sheet and steer the cart towards the items on your list.

---

* While shopping with you, your child not only develops observation skills, but also feels useful and needed by carrying out an important task.

55

Doll House

To create a room for a doll, you will need a large cardboard box and a few small pieces of material like buttons, corks, coloured paper, scissors and glue. Together with your child, glue the coloured paper in the bottom of the box. A matchbox could be used to make a bed, a cork as a pillow and a piece of thicker material for a blanket. Create a dresser by gluing a few matchboxes together. Find ways with your child to further decorate the room. Both of you will certainly have a lot of ideas.

** Hones manual skills, releases creativity and imagination.

56
Telephone

To begin the game, get a group of children together and have them sit down side by side. One after another, each child whispers a message to the next, like 'Dogs are barking outside'. The last child in line says the sentence aloud. The fun is seeing how much the whispered phrase has changed to become 'Hogs are parking a ride'.

---

*   A group activity that generate a lot of joy and laughter.

57

Rattle Around

Pour a handful of rice into an empty yogurt container and use a piece of paper to cover the top and secure it in place with a rubber band — stretching the paper as tightly as possible. Now use wallpaper adhesive to help your child glue tiny pieces of paper to the outside of the rattle. The rattle has to dry before it can be played.

* Making this toy with you brings your child a lot of happiness.
  Another benefit is the development of manual skills.

58

Cat and Mouse

Before the cat begins to chase mice, tell the children how the mice can escape the cat's sharp claws: by touching an object made of, for example, wood, metal or plastic. If the children are playing outside, they can huddle around a tree, grab a branch or sit on a wooden bench. If a mouse fails to 'escape' in this way, it will be caught and becomes the cat in the next game.

---

*   A variation on a traditional game that develops a child's powers of observation and reflexes; also releases a lot of emotion.

59

Wind Vane

Give your child stiff paper in the shape of a square and ask her to come up with an idea for decorating it. When she is finished, cut the square as indicated on the illustration above. Fold down the loose corners, secure them with a pin and affix this to a stick. When your child blows, the windmill will start to turn...again, and again.

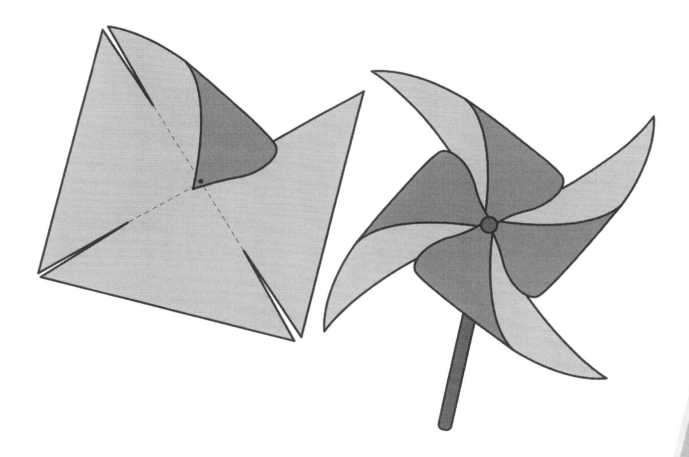

---

* Develops your child's creativity as well as allows her to discover the power of her own lungs.

60

The Shape of Me

Lay out a large sheet of paper on the floor and ask your child to lie down on it. Draw an outline of his shape and then cut it out together. Let your child draw in eyes, a nose and a mouth. Maybe your child can draw some clothes on the body? Maybe she prefers a witch's costume or tiger stripes? Ask and help if needed.

** A game that teaches control of one's body, exercises manual dexterity and develops creativity.

61
Rocking Horse

Ask your child to sit down on the floor, pull his knees to his chest and hold them tightly with his arms. Now the 'horse' begins to rock — first forwards and backwards, then left and right. If your child is willing to try, help him to rock far enough forward and backward that his head touches the floor. Then return to the starting position.

** Thanks to this activity, your child practises balance and learns the capabilities of his or her body.

62
A Fine Line

Draw a few animals on pieces of cardboard paper, for example, a cat without whiskers, a hedgehog without spines or a dog without a tail. Ask your child to identify and draw in the missing elements. Don't forget to praise the finished work!

** An activity that develops manual dexterity and gives a child the satisfaction of working independently.

63

A Present for My Grandparents

Prepare two Clementine oranges, edible cloves and two coloured ribbons. Before beginning this activity, show your child the cloves — their appearance, colour and smell — then explain what cloves are used for. Wrap each orange in a criss-crossed ribbon (see the illustration above) and tie them in a bow. Then ask your child to puncture the skin of the oranges with cloves.

* Good practise for hand muscles and exposure to unusual scents.

64

Motor Mouths: Start Your Engines!

All parents know that their children sometimes have an uncontrollable urge to...talk. This activity should satisfy even the most talkative kids. The rules are simple: at your signal ask your child to say as many words as possible; all topics are allowed, but using made-up words or repeating words is not. Each round lasts 10 seconds (measure time with a stopwatch that your child can see). As you will notice, this game isn't so easy!

**   An excellent game with language; hones reflexes and concentration and forces your child to exercise his mental acuity against the clock.

65

What's the Time, Mr. Wolf?

One child is chosen as the 'Wolf'. He stands with his back to the rest of the children, who line up about 20 feet away behind their 'safety start line'. The children call out: "What's the time, Mr. Wolf?" He turns and calls out a time, such as 'three o'clock' and then turns his back again. The children take three steps forward — the number of steps should correspond with the time he calls. To score a point, the children must cross the 'Wolf's line'. Play proceeds and the children gradually creep closer to the line where the Wolf is standing. When they have almost reached him, he turns and calls: "Dinnertime!" He then chases the others back, aiming to capture one child before he or she crosses the start line. The child who is caught becomes the next wolf.

* Reinforces learning about counting and telling time as well as gives children practise in following rules and playing together.

66

Memory

Together with your child, remove all of the jacks, queens, kings and aces from a deck of cards. Lay them out on a table so that your child can see each of these cards clearly. The game begins when you turn the cards face down. Taking turns, each of you chooses two cards. If these make a pair, for example two kings, the lucky player places these two cards aside and chooses two more cards. If the two cards are different, put them back in place. The challenge is remembering where each card is to avoid making mistakes on the next turn. The winner is the player who finds the most pairs.

✱✱ Your child learns to look closely and develops memory skills.

67

Dog Bowl

To prepare this bowl, you will need some colour magazines, water and glue as well as a bowl to use as a mould. Ask your child to rip the paper into pieces and put them into the container of water and glue — he or she will definitely enjoy this part! First wrap the mould in the wet paper and leave it to dry for a few days. When the paper is hard, remove the mould and decorate the bowl with a bow.

** During this activity your child gains manual dexterity and develops artistic creativity.

68

On the Farm

Choose one child to be the farmer's wife and let the other children work out amongst themselves which animal each wants to be. Have the children sit on a bench. Then the farmer (that's you!) comes out to ask his 'wife' whether they have a chicken, for example, on their farm. If she says 'yes', the animal that was named has to run around the bench before the farmer can catch him or her and return to the same spot on the bench. If the animal is caught, that child plays the part of the farmer in the next round.

** Good practise for speed and reflexes.

69

Set the Table

Once again colour magazines will come in handy for this activity. But that's not all! With your child prepare paper plates and napkins, plastic cutlery and glue. Cut out pictures of fruit, vegetables, cookies, ice cream, cake and anything else that can be served to guests at a party. Glue these pictures onto the plates and then set the table — show your child where to put the cutlery and napkins. You could also decorate the table using, for example, paper flowers. Let the party begin!

* Thanks to this game, your child uses the imagination and practises manual dexterity as well as learns how to set a table.

70
Magic Blanket

Every house has at least one old blanket that can be used for a game. Have your child stand on the blanket and shuffle forward or slide as if ice-skating. Have him lie down on his stomach and push himself along with arms and legs as if pretending to ride a sled or spin in a circle like on a carrousel. Maybe your child will invent a different way to move?

---

*   This is a fantastic physical activity that develops a child's imagination.

71

Pick Me Up

Gather beads or crayons. Spread them out on the floor, but not too far away from one another. Take turns collecting the ones that are touching — one or two at a time. Once there are only individual objects left, only one can be picked up per turn. The loser is the one who is left with the last object at the end of the game.

** A simple game of strategy that teaches logical thinking.

72
Nature Walk

During a walk in the park or through the forest, collect different leaves and flowers with your child. Name each one of them and point out each plant's characteristic features. Back at home put the plants into a book, each one separately, and wait a few days until they are dry. Then glue them onto pieces of paper, place the paper into plastic sheaths and organise your protected specimens into a binder. Now you have an album!

---

* Your child learns the names of plants and begins to appreciate nature as well as develops manual dexterity.

73

Hot & Cold

Ask your child to leave the room; hide an object and then invite her to return and search for it. To make it easier, give your child a hint for finding the hidden treasure. Your hints should be encoded: for example, 'The object is next to...' You can also help your child by saying 'hot' or 'cold' when the child is getting closer or farther away, respectively, from the hidden object.

---

* An interesting game that is well liked by children; develops the powers of observation and teaches logical and more precise thinking.

74

Stamp the Snowman

Draw the outlines of a snowman on a piece of paper and let your child use a cork (e.g. from a wine bottle) dipped in paint to stamp the snowman with colour. Each part of the snowman — the hat, broom or buttons — will require a different cork and colour of paint. When your child finishes working, glue the paper onto a larger piece of paper and cut the second paper to make a frame. This drawing can be mounted on a corkboard in your child's room. In the same way, you can also make a picture with flowers or another theme.

* Teaches accuracy, manual dexterity and develops a sense of aesthetics.

75

Dogs or Tigers

This is a very simple, well-known game that doesn't require any accessories. Get down on hands and knees and chase one another: first the little dog runs away from the larger dog and then vice versa. You can also play at being tigers that wrestle, roll around and climb on one another, etc.

---

*   Excellent physical exercise for children and adults. Creates a lot of joy and strengthens family ties.

76

Full Circle

Prepare a large plastic cup, a few pieces of coloured paper and glue. Turn the cup upside down on the paper and trace around the rim to create a circle. Make a total of five circles in this way. Cut them all out and then cut each circle in half. After mixing them up, pull out a random half circle and ask your child to find a missing piece of another colour. Together your halves create a two-toned circle. Glue these colourful circles on a piece of white paper to create an intriguing picture.

** Creative play —— preparing a picture in pop-art style. Also teaches your child to recognise geometric figures and colours.

77

Indian!

Recite a fragment of a poem that your child knows aloud and at the same time move your hand quickly against your open mouth like Indians from the Sioux tribe. Your voice will resemble their famous cries. Your child will have to listen carefully in order to guess the poem and then he can finish it in the same way.

WAH!
WHOA!
WAH!
WHOA!

** Teaches your child how to listen carefully.

78
Toes to and fro

Ask the children to lie down on the floor with legs out and bare feet, stretching out their toes as wide as possible. The child who stretches out his or her toes the widest is the winner. Finally, lead the children through this relaxation exercise: ask them to rotate their ankles in a circle, first in one direction, then the other.

*A very good exercise for a child's feet.

79

Foot Massage

This is a great activity for the beach. Put water and a little bit of sand into a plastic bottle, but do not cap it. Sit next to your child and show him how to roll the bottle along the sole of his bare feet, mixing the water and sand inside the bottle. Let the contents of the bottle settle and then start over. Once all the water has spilled out, your child can begin the game again by adding more water.

✻✻   A game that helps to counteract flat-footedness.

80

Poor Puppy

This is a game that can be played when your child has a friend over to play. One child imitates a dog in a bad mood: walking around on 'four paws', barking dejectedly and making sad faces, looking silly all the while. The second child tries to comfort the 'animal' by petting its head and talking to it kindly: "Oh, poor puppy! What happened?" By laughing the second child loses and becomes the dog in the next round.

---

* Develops a child's inborn acting ability and teaches emotional control.

81
Playdough Cake

When you are baking a cake, propose your child the opportunity to 'bake' her own. You will need different colours of playdough and paper as well as raisins, nuts or coloured sprinkles. First have your child make three round cake layers, placing them on top of one another. Sprinkle the cake with pieces of coloured paper and the edible decorations. Before beginning this activity, dress your child in an apron. Bon appétit!

   ✱   A good exercise for manual dexterity and the imagination.

82

Have a Ball

This outdoor game involves a ball that your child pushes through an obstacle course. Use first and foremost natural obstacles such as trees, bushes, rocks and sticks. Depending on the terrain and your child's physical abilities, the ball can be large or small, heavy or light.

** This game contributes to your child's overall physical fitness and allows him or her to practise precise movements.

83

Take a Break…

After a long interval of play, every child needs to rest. Ask your child to lie down on his or her back on a carpeted floor, rug or exercise mat. With arms extended, knees bent and eyes closed, ask your child to bring both legs to one side and, after a moment of rest, to the other. Finally, have your child straighten and stretch both legs. That feels good!

***

* An activity that is sure to relax your child!

84

What's under There?

Prepare a variety of different colourful objects, e.g. a toy car, teddy bear, plastic cup or bowl. Lay them out on the floor and ask your child to look at and try to remember the objects. Cover everything with a blanket and ask your child to talk about what is underneath. Start by covering only two or three toys. If your child has no problem describing the hidden objects, start adding more. You might also ask your child to describe the colour of the objects.

** Develops a child's memory and ability to concentrate as well as describe objects.

85

Cat, Mice & Tunnel

This is a game for at least three children. One child, the cat, chases the other children, who are mice. If the cat manages to touch a mouse, that child stands still with legs apart. If another mouse crawls through the frozen mouse's legs without being caught by the cat, the mouse is unfrozen. When the cat is tired of catching mice or if all of the mice have been caught, the game is finished.

* Teaches children to help each other and trains reflexes.

86
Paper Ribbon

Prepare different colours of tissue paper, scissors and a ribbon. Cut five discs of tissue paper with a thickness of about half an inch, each in a different colour, and ask your child to pull the ends apart, creating a long strip of paper. Twist one set of paper ends together to create a small handle, leaving the rest free. Bind the handle together with a ribbon, but not too tight to tear through the paper. These long ribbons can be used as an accessory by girls when pretending to be a ballet dancer or gymnast.

** Develops manual dexterity, physical coordination and creativity.

Gather Round

Show your child a round object and then find other objects together that have the same shape. Ask your child to hold and examine each object as well as try to name what it is. Put all of these objects into a bag and throw in other objects with triangular or rectangular shapes. Now let your child reach into the bag and by touch alone pull out only the round objects. You can do the same thing with the triangular and rectangular objects.

** An activity that teaches a child about geometric forms as well as hones the sense of touch.

88
Same Difference

Use this idea the next time you need to keep your child busy during a long car or train trip. Think up a short but interesting story and begin telling it. From time to time, incorporate the same words into the story. You can also repeat random words that come into your head, for example the names of animals, fruit, vegetables, colours, seasons, etc. Your child should react when you repeat a word.

* A good exercise for practising listening and concentration skills as well as reflexes.

89

Target Practise

Place a plastic bucket or box on the floor. A few steps away lay out a piece of coloured string to mark the starting line. Now ask your child to stand behind the line, take a ball and try to throw it into the bucket or box. If your child succeeds, move the line a little bit farther away to increase the difficulty. For every successful throw give your child a button. After winning five buttons, award your child a special prize, such as a favourite fruit.

***   Trains dexterity and accustoms a child to the idea of winning and losing.

90

Ducks, Swallows and Trees

Ask a group of children to pretend to be animals and plants that live in the country. The ducks walk, waddling from side to side and turning their heads left and right, as if ruffling their feathers. They can also look for food — squatting down and leaning forward as if pecking at seeds. Swallows stand on one leg, extending the other leg behind them and arms spread wide. Trees stand with legs apart and arms raised, swaying from side to side as if blown in the wind. The children can also choose to imitate other animals.

* A game that helps children develop balance and physical fitness.

91
Drawing Lines

Ask your child to cut out a few different houses using coloured paper and glue them onto a piece of white paper — with your assistance if necessary. Then, using a large marker, ask your child to draw a path from house to house. Draw the first line, if needed, as an example. Your child can also describe the colours and shapes of each house.

** A good exercise to practise concentration and precision.

92
Object Lesson

Hide a few different objects (e.g. a block, spoon, crayon, newspaper, bottle cap, etc.) under a clean towel or dishtowel. Lay out a matching set of objects in front of your child, showing and naming each one. Then ask your child to find the hidden object that matches.

* This game can also be adapted to incorporate food (fruits and vegetables) — a good way for your child to learn how to identify and name them.

93

Crepe

Ask your child to lie down on his back on the floor. Tell him he is a crepe and you have to spread a topping over him. Ask your child if he wants to be a crepe with jam or syrup. In the first case, use your hands to rub your child, starting with the face and ending on the feet; if the latter, use your fingers to tap all over your child's body. Now you have to roll the crepe up by pushing the child onto his side, then stomach (in this position your child should brace himself using his hands and slightly raise his head), to the other side and again on his back. Your child can roll on his own once he has the hang of it.

---

*   Excellent exercise for your child as well as an opportunity
    to strengthen your relationship through touch.

94

Happy Cloud, Sad Cloud

Have your child stand in front of a mirror, first making a happy face and then a sad face. Each time ask her to take a good look at her own expression. Then ask your child to draw happy and sad faces on a piece of white paper on which you have drawn cloud outlines. She can also draw in rain next to the sad clouds or a sun next to the happy clouds.

** Strengthens understanding of the concepts 'happy' and 'sad' as well as develops manual dexterity.

95

Weather Calendar

Take two pieces of drawing paper. On one write the names of the week and create a chart underneath. On the second, draw a variety of symbols to represent weather conditions: sun, clouds, a sun partly hidden by clouds, a storm cloud, rain, snow, etc. Encourage your child to observe the weather every day and glue the correct weather symbol on the calendar for each day.

* Your child learns to observe nature and recognise atmospheric phenomena.

Time to Rhyme

Every child knows and enjoys rhymes — one of the best kinds of fun! Here are some examples of rhymes that you can say or sing along with your child:

Twinkle, twinkle, little star,
How I wonder what you are!
Up above the world so high
Like a diamond in the sky,
Twinkle, twinkle, little star,
How I wonder what you are!

Hey, diddle, diddle!
The cat and the fiddle,
The cow jumped over the moon;
The little dog laughed
To see such sport,
And the dish ran away with the spoon.

* These simple rhymes hone your child's listening skills, memory and pronunciation.

97

Outlines

Look through coloured magazines and cut out figures of people or animals. Ask your child to place these one by one on a piece of paper and trace around them with a large marker. When the cut out is taken away, the child's traced figure remains. It might not be perfect, but allow your child to practise to create more accurate contours.

---

* Your child learns to draw figures and hones his manual dexterity.

98
Painting on Glass

Prepare a tube of toothpaste and ask your child to sit in front of a mirror — ideally a large hallway mirror. Ask your child to take a closer look at his or her face. Point out its symmetry: eyebrows, eyes, nose, cheeks and ears. Then ask your child to use the toothpaste to recreate this reflection on the glass. No child can resist this invitation!

---

* A game that helps children to remember their own image.

99

Shoe in to Win

The children's task is to put shoes on the legs of a chair as fast as possible. Prepare as many shoes as there are chair legs. When you say 'go!' the children leap into action. The child who puts shoes on his or her chair first wins.

---

*   A good activity to practise speed and manual dexterity.

100
Name that Fruit

Draw the outlines of fruit on a piece of paper: e.g. apples, pears and bananas. Allow your child to choose the appropriate crayons to fill in the figures. Now describe each fruit in turn: its shape and colour (e.g. 'It is yellow and is shaped like a croissant', i.e. a banana). Ask your child to guess which fruit you are talking about by saying its name and pointing to the drawing. Another variant of this game: place a selection of fruit on a plate and ask your child to select the right fruit as you describe it.

*** Teaches careful listening, association and observation skills.

101

Whose Nose is This?

This is a game for at least three children. Blindfold each child in turn with a small towel, scarf or handkerchief and see if he or she can recognise friends just by touching parts of their faces: nose, ears, hair, shoulders, etc.

*** A great exercise for increasing a child's sensitivity to touch —— and a lot of fun and giggles for the kids involved.

Contents

Printed in Great Britain
by Amazon